"THE WORLD'S EASIEST POCKET GUIDE"

— TO —

Starting Your First Savings Plan

"THE WORLD'S EASIEST POCKET GUIDE"

TO

Starting Your First Savings Plan

LARRY BURKETT
WITH ED STRAUSS
ILLUSTRATED BY KEN SAVE

MOODY PRESS
CHICAGO

For Lightwave Publishing
Managing Editor: *Rick Osborne*
Project Assistant: *Mikal Marrs*
Text Director: *Christie Bowler*
Art Director: *Terry van Roon*

Text & Illustrations © 2001 BURKETT & KIDS, LLC
Executive Producer: *Allen Burkett*

All rights reserved. No part of this book may be reproduced in any form without permission in writing from the publisher, except in the case of brief quotations embodied in critical articles or reviews.

All Scripture quotations, unless otherwise indicated, are taken from the *Holy Bible, New International Version*®. NIV®. Copyright ©1973, 1978, 1984 by International Bible Society. Used by permission of Zondervan Publishing House. All rights reserved.

ISBN: 0-8024-0996-2

1 3 5 7 9 10 8 6 4 2

Printed in the United States of America

Table of Contents

How to Use This Book 6

Chapter 1
The Need for Savings 7

Chapter 2
Our Nonsaving Society 13

Chapter 3
Mapping a Savings Plan 19

Chapter 4
Setting Up a Savings Account 27

Chapter 5
Short-Term Savings 33

Chapter 6
Long-Term Savings 37

Chapter 7
Saving for Emergencies 45

Chapter 8
Nickels and Dimes 51

Chapter 9
Sticking to Your Plan 55

Chapter 10
The Payoff 59

Glossary 62

Index 63

How to Use This Book

Shortly after leaving home, many teens and young adults embark on a learning curve so drastic that it resembles a roller-coaster ride. Things they never did before—such as holding down a full-time job, paying bills, saving money, renting an apartment, using a credit card—suddenly become sink-or-swim survival skills. Most people fail to learn these basics while still at home and are woefully unprepared for life in the real world when they move out on their own.

The first four books in this series—*Getting Your First Credit Card, Buying Your First Car, Renting Your First Apartment,* and *Preparing for College*—were written to teach you the basic life skills you need to survive in today's jungle. In these four new books, *Your First Full-Time Job, Your First Savings Plan, Your First Investment,* and *Your First Financial Plan,* we walk you step-by-step through getting and keeping a job, saving money, investing money without losing your shirt, and getting and keeping control of your money.

These books contain a wealth of commonsense tips. They also give sound advice from a godly, biblical perspective. It is our prayer that the books in this series will save you from having to learn these things in the "school of hard knocks."

To get the most out of these books, you should photocopy and complete the checklists and forms we've included. We provided them to help you take on these new tasks step-by-step and to make these books as practical as possible.

Each book contains a glossary to explain commonly used terms. If at any point while reading you need a clear definition of a certain word or term, you can look it up. Each book also contains a helpful index that allows you to find pages where a key word or subject is mentioned in the book.

CHAPTER 1

The Need for Savings

The Need for Savings

Go to the Ant

Have you ever sat down beside an anthill—not on *top* of it, please!—and watched the busy little ants carry grain, sticks, or pieces of dead things up the slope of their great metropolis, then disappear down into the labyrinth below with their find? Ever wonder why they never cease working, except when a guard stops them to feel their antennae and check their ant ID?

When you consider how small an ant's brain is, it's astonishing that they *know* they need to store up food for winter. Obviously, since there's not much room in their craniums for creative thinking, God must have hardwired those instructions into them. That frees up the remaining brain cells to think about how to get back home with the goods.

Proverbs 6:6, 8 says, "Go to the ant, you sluggard; consider its ways and be wise! . . . It stores its provisions in summer and gathers its food at harvest." The ant stores food knowing a time will come when she will need it. And what does God say about the ant? She is *wise!* Wanna be wise? "Go to the ant."

But some Christians can stare at an anthill for hours, then walk away muttering that God's people should never save money. They say it's greedy. They point to needy causes in the world—helping the poor, supporting missionaries—and say that any extra money we have should be immediately put to use in God's kingdom. That *sounds* spiritual, but is it right?

Is there any scriptural justification for saving money instead of immediately giving away every penny? Yes, there is. The Bible indicates that it is godly wisdom to set part of your surplus aside for future needs. If God touches your heart to give to a specific need, do so. A tender heart is a gift from God. But so is wisdom, and following the ant's example is wise.

Does the Bible indicate that it is wise to save, that planning pays off? Yes. "By wisdom a house is built, and through understanding it is established; through knowledge its rooms are filled with rare and beautiful treasures" (Proverbs 24:3–4). So the good news is that you can open a savings account and still be a Christian.

Saving Vs. Hoarding

We are to save, but we're *not* to save far more than we need. That's hoarding. A classic example of this is the rich fool in Luke 12:16–21 who had a huge harvest and no room to store it. He didn't want to share it with the poor and needy, so he decided to tear down his barns and build larger ones to hoard it. He then planned to retire and enjoy life. Bad choice! He died that night.

Jesus said, "Watch out! Be on your guard against all kinds of greed; a man's life does not consist in the abundance of his possessions" (Luke 12:15). Jesus also said, "Do not store up for yourselves [hoard] treasures on earth, where moth and rust destroy, and where thieves break in and steal" (Matthew 6:19).

Hoarding shows a lack of trust in God. It shows we are trusting in our wealth and material possessions to meet our needs. Paul tells Timothy in 1 Timothy 6:17–18 to command Christians *not* to "put their hope in wealth, which is so uncertain, but to put their hope in God, who richly provides us with everything for our enjoyment. Command them to do good, to be rich in good deeds, and to be generous and willing to share." So save for needs, set aside for specific goals, but don't hoard wealth for a sense of security.

Anthill Cutbacks

There is a distinct difference between hoarding and saving. As Proverbs 6:6–8 says, during the harvest months an ant gathers the food she will need during the winter months. Note, she puts aside only what she'll need.

An anthill was moved from New England to Florida. The first year the ants steadily gathered and stored food—but winter never came. The next year the ants cut back on the food they stored. After winter didn't come the third year, the ants quit storing food. They stored food in their chambers to meet a specific need. When the need was gone, they stopped storing.

Saving is common sense. It is a hedge against future needs. But hoarding is a lack of trust. The difference is attitude. So you see, ants are not only wise, they've also got *attitude*.

Reasons to Save

OK, so you're not going to stash your money inside an anthill. Neither are you going to hoard it like Ebenezer Scrooge or the rich fool. But there are two very good reasons to save money: The first is that if you set money aside for specific needs, it will be there when you need it.

The second reason is that money in a savings account gathers interest. You are putting your money to work for you. It appreciates (increases) in value! The Bible advises putting money in the bank to gather interest. In Jesus' Parable of the Talents, the master told his servant, "You should have put my money on deposit with the bankers, so that when I returned I would have received it back with interest" (Matthew 25:27).

OK, you agree that saving is a necessary thing. But what needs should Christians save money for?

- *Getting out of debt:* Debt is a hungry beast that will try to devour you. If you have debts, it is vital to get rid of them. The first step is to stop getting into more debt. How? Rein in your spending habits and stay within a budget before the beast devours you. You simply must set aside money and get those debts paid.

- *Short-term expenses:* A short-term expense is something you have to save for a few weeks or months to buy. You decide what a short-term expense should be. If you need a new couch or want a new leather jacket, a stereo, or some other not-so-expensive (but not-so-cheap) item, you must save for it. It's *not* wise to purchase it on credit or installment plan—you end up paying more than it's worth.

- *Long-term expenses:* Long-term expenses are things for which you must save for a couple of years, many years, or even your whole life! Examples are . . .

1. *Buying a car:* This is one of the biggest expenses you will face as a young adult. You can pick up a junker for a few hundred dollars, but on the average a good used car costs a whopping $10,000. Saving for it ahead of time could mean not paying $1–2,000 in interest.

2. *College education:* College is very expensive! The average cost of a four-year college degree is $40,000. If you think God wants you to go to college, but you give all your money away to charities (or spend it all), well, the charities and shops will love you, but guess what? You won't be going to college. Or if you do, you'll end up paying thousands more for it.

3. *Getting married:* Most of us eventually get married, but there's a price tag attached to the rings and rice and receptions. That picture-perfect moment costs money. And once you have kids, you need to provide for them—you have to think like an ant, so why not get a jump on it and start now?

4. *Buying a house:* This is *the* biggie! Houses are very expensive, and you'll need to pay around $10,000 minimum up front for a typical down payment—let alone keep up your mortgage payments later.

5. *Retirement:* You will get old one day. I know it's hard to believe, but it *will* happen. You may not think right now that it's worth saving money for retirement, but you'll have a different viewpoint when you're sixty-eight. Guaranteed. But by then it will be too late. So start now.

Make a Start

Make a list of things you need to save for, from new shin pads to a guitar to an education to retirement. Then estimate how much each will cost. This will give you an idea of what your saving needs are. Photocopy and use the following list.

Don't let the total overwhelm you. We will explain these various categories in greater detail in later chapters and show you how it *can* be done.

SHORT-TERM SAVINGS	COST
1. Clothing	$
2. Christmas Presents	$
3. Other	$
4. Other	$
5. Other	$
6. Other	$
7. Other	$

LONG-TERM SAVINGS	COST
1. Car	$
2. College (education)	$
3. Wedding	$
4. Job Loss Funds	$
5. Urgent Giving	$
7. Buying a Home	$
8. Retirement	$
9. Other	$

TOTAL $

CHAPTER 2
Our Nonsaving Society

Our Nonsaving Society

Spending Every Penny

In the last chapter we listed reasons for saving money, whether you keep it in a bank or stuff it in a sock under your bed. Opening a savings account makes more sense, because your money collects interest instead of dust bunnies.

Sad to say, saving is a foreign concept to most people these days. Most don't set aside even a small part of their earnings. They have no inclination to do so. Their motto is, "If I have money, I'll spend it." This attitude is summed up in the verse, "Let us eat and drink . . . for tomorrow we die" (Isaiah 22:13). Or to give that a modern twist, "Eat, drink, and be merry, 'cause you're only young once!"

The results? Most "young once" people spend all their money on the latest brand-name clothes, state-of-the-art stereos, CDs, and going out with friends. They don't save one penny. If they *have* a savings account, they treat it like a backup checking account, there to dip into when checking is empty.

Pooh, Jabar, and Joseph

Want a picture of how most people treat savings accounts? Think of Winnie the Pooh gorging himself on honey. "In the house of the wise are stores of choice food and oil, but a foolish man devours all he has" (Proverbs 21:20). Or take Karim Abdul Jabar. He played longer than anyone in NBA history, earning close to $100 million in his career. But when he left the NBA he had nothing and owed a huge amount of taxes to boot.

On the other hand we have Joseph: When he knew that seven years of famine were coming to Egypt, he didn't say, "Let's enjoy the surplus now. I'll wait till just before the famine and *then* I'll save some grain. I promise." Nope. Joseph got busy immediately and saved up enough grain to feed the entire land of Egypt during the famine. (See Genesis 41:48–49.) He collected so much grain that he was able to sell the surplus to surrounding nations at a profit! (See Genesis 41:57.)

Four thousand years ago, Joseph had more wisdom than one hundred million modern Americans. Compare his overflowing granaries to today's penniless purses, vacant wallets, overdrawn checking accounts, and empty savings accounts. Ah, the joy of coming of age in the new millennium!

Credit Cards and Lemmings

As if a bankrupt entry into adulthood wasn't bad enough, the new rage is the debt entrance! Ladies and gentlemen, we are talking about the credit card, the marvel that allows millions of teens, fresh out of high school, to leap into debt like lemmings flinging their furry little selves off the top of a fjord into the frozen sea below.

To get the full scoop on credit cards, see the book in this series, *Getting Your First Credit Card*. We will only touch on its perils here. (Whoa! Look out for falling lemmings!)

First, you need to know that credit cards in themselves are not bad. Many people—particularly businesspeople—use credit cards responsibly and for good purposes. The big damage happens when people use credit irresponsibly and rack up charges they can't pay at the end of the month. They then end up paying humongous interest charges—18 or even 28 percent—on debts they incur.

Worst of all, this doesn't happen just once or twice. This is not some minor once-in-a-lifetime oversight. Fully half of Americans who own credit cards carry an unpaid balance—and pay interest on it for months or even years. It's not an occasional slipup; it's a way of life.

Buying on Credit (Don't!)

Just in case you're not completely convinced that saving is a must, let's take a look at some of the results of *not* saving. What happens if you *don't* save the money? What happens if you take out a loan to buy these things or use your credit card to purchase them? (Think lemmings.)

If you have debts, whether bank loans or credit card charges, you are paying interest on those debts and that interest can range from 9 percent to a whopping 28 percent. You won't just have to pay back the principal (original amount you borrowed). The longer you take to repay the loan, the more you pay in interest charges. You could charge $2,000 on a card and end up paying nearly $3,000 back! (See the charts on pages 35–36 of the book in this series, *Getting Your First Credit Card*.) Just think what you could have done with that extra $1,000!

If possible, never take out a loan or pull out your credit card. But if you already *have* debts, pay them off as soon as possible. "Let no debt remain outstanding" (Romans 13:8). That means putting the brakes on unnecessary expenses and saving money. (Now is *not* the time to start double-tithing or to pledge $200 for a new sidewalk in front of your church.)

But what if you're minding your own business, walking down the street, and you suddenly see the deal of the century in a store window? It could be a $299 couch that you *sort of* actually need, or a $399 stereo that you don't need, but *really, really* want. Either way, you're standing there looking at the price tag with 14¢ in your pocket and $19.72 in your savings. Times like this, the temptation to pull out your credit card can be nearly overwhelming.

But remember: "No temptation has seized you except what is common to man. . . . But when you are tempted, [God] will also provide a way out so that you can stand up under it" (1 Corinthians 10:13). Often, the "way out" is making the commitment that you are going to *save* money, not spend it. So keep your card in your wallet and walk away.

Step Aside, Wyatt Earp

It used to be that when hardworking Americans needed to buy something that cost more than they could afford—say a newfangled Buffalo radio—they scrimped and saved and set the money aside in a glass jar, cookie tin, or bank account. When they had enough, they went to the store, plunked down the cash, bought their Buffalo, and took it home.

Back then, the virtues of patience, hard work, and thrift were deeply ingrained in American culture. Things had *value* because people had to cut corners and squirrel away money dime by dime, in order to buy them. It was a long time before they forgot all the treats they had denied themselves in order to save up some serious spending money.

These days, most lemmings . . . I mean, people . . . don't seem to either *know* or *care* what things cost. They don't realize they'll have to work hard to pay off their debts. They turn on the shopping channel, see a new exercise bike for a mere $39.99 a month, and whip their credit card out faster than Wyatt Earp slapping leather down at the O.K. Corral.

Ho! Only $39.99 a month? Anybody can afford *that*. They don't care if they end up paying $39.99 a month for a whole year, with $148 of that being interest charges, not to mention paying $41.66 to the credit card company in late charges. I mean, how hard can it *be* to pick up the phone, dial the 1-800 number, and read the little numbers off your credit card? Not hard. How hard is it to grasp that you'll end up paying *far* more for that flab blaster than any possible use you will *ever* get out of it? Harder.

When you save your money first, then wait for a sale on the item you want, you always get a better deal—and have a greater appreciation of its worth. "Buy now" is rushed and costs more. In fact, even if you finally buy that item at the regular price, you *still* save money!—because you avoid paying those high interest and finance charges.

The lesson? Saving saves! Credit corrupts! And absolute credit corrupts absolutely. (Ask someone who's maxed out a credit card with a $50,000 limit. Ouch!)

Personal Case History

Now it's time to do some painful self-examination and find out where you're at right now. Discover just how much you're spending—most of it thoughtlessly. Track your spending for a couple of months on a sheet of paper set up something like this. It might convince you of the need to save.

Date:	Item:	Amount:
_____	_____	$_____
_____	_____	$_____
_____	_____	$_____

Ouch! Look at that money flowing through your fingers! But you're not done yet. Pick up a pen, roll up your sleeves, and list all your debts.

Money owed to:	Amount:	
Parents	$_____	
Friends	$_____	
Former friends	$_____	(They still want their money)
Credit card(s)	$_____	
Dept. store cards	$_____	
Bank (for auto)	$_____	
Installment plans	$_____	(Buy now, pay lots later)
Other _____	$_____	
Other _____	$_____	
Other _____	$_____	
TOTAL	**$_____**	

By doing these two simple tasks, hopefully you can see that, by not saving, at least five bad things can happen: (1) You spend every penny. (2) You buy on credit. (3) You don't have money for emergencies or other things that come up. (4) You end up in debt. And (5) you end up paying more for whatever you buy.

But if you can get control of that thoughtless spending you can break the cycle. Ready? Read on.

CHAPTER 3
Mapping a Savings Plan

Mapping a Savings Plan

Gotta Have a Budget

Ever sat down and added up how much you earned in a year, and then been surprised that all that money has run through your fingers like so much water, with little to show for it? Ever wonder why?

Part of the problem is that you might have a "gotta have" attitude. You simply "gotta have" the latest clothes, your own cell phone, the newest CD, and you "gotta see" the latest "two thumbs up—way up" movie, etc. But there is one *gotta have* that you simply *gotta* have before any other *gotta have,* and that is a budget.

Simply put, a budget is a written list of what you plan to do with your money. It's about deciding how much money you want to spend and what you will spend it on, *before* you spend it: for example, how much you'll give to God, how much you'll save for the future, and how much you'll spend on things you need. It's about how much you'll have fun with—and not spending a penny more when that's gone. See the budget form on the next page.

Here's how to get the most out of this form: Since fine-tuning a budget will take a bit of practice, photocopy the *Monthly Income & Expenses* page so you have copies to "practice" on; then keep it handy, ready to fill in. In the next few chapters we discuss each category. (If you already have your budget figured out, go ahead and fill in the form.)

Every day brings opportunities to buy something you hadn't planned on buying. If you have no budget, chances are good you'll cave in to the temptation. But if you have a budget, you'll know even before your hand hits your wallet whether you can afford that "gotta have" item or not. (Yes, we are talking *that* quick.)

OK, let's take a closer look at the categories on this form.

Monthly Income & Expenses

Annual Income _____
Monthly Income _____

LESS
1. **Charitable Giving** _____
2. **Tax** _____

NET SPENDABLE INCOME _____

3. **Housing (30%)** _____
   - Mortgage (Rent) _____
   - Insurance _____
   - Taxes _____
   - Electricity _____
   - Gas _____
   - Water _____
   - Sanitation _____
   - Telephone _____
   - Maintenance _____
   - Other _____

4. **Food (17%)** _____

5. **Auto(s) (15%)** _____
   - Payments _____
   - Gas & Oil _____
   - Insurance _____
   - License _____
   - Taxes _____
   - Maint/Repair/ Replacement _____

6. **Insurance (5%)** _____
   - Life _____
   - Medical _____
   - Other _____

7. **Debts (5%)** _____
   - Credit Cards _____
   - Loans & Notes _____
   - Other _____

8. **Enter. / Recreation (7%)** _____
   - Eating Out _____
   - Trips _____
   - Baby-Sitters _____
   - Activities _____
   - Vacation _____
   - Other _____

9. **Clothing (5%)** _____

10. **Savings (5%)** _____

11. **Medical Expenses (5%)** _____
    - Doctor _____
    - Dental _____
    - Drugs _____
    - Other _____

12. **Miscellaneous (6%)** _____
    - Toiletry, Cosmetics _____
    - Beauty, Barber _____
    - Laundry, Cleaning _____
    - Allowances, Lunches _____
    - Subscriptions, Gifts _____
      (Incl. Christmas)
    - Special Education _____
    - Cash _____
    - Other _____

TOTAL EXPENSES _____

Net Spendable Income _____

Difference _____

Pay the Lord

The very first dollar figure on your budget, even before paying taxes, is Charitable Giving. This means giving to God, the source of all blessing and supply. Giving back a portion of your income to God shows that you recognize that everything you have comes from Him, that you are merely a steward of the things you have in your possession. You're just managing them for God. As 1 Chronicles 29:14 says, "Everything comes from you, and we have given you only what comes from your hand."

For many Christians, Charitable Giving means tithing 10 percent of their income to God, whether they give it all to their church, or send part of it to missionaries. For others, 10 percent is merely the starting place for giving, not the end. Even if you don't believe in tithing, the New Testament is jam-packed with verses that admonish believers to open their hearts and wallets and give to their church, to missions, to the poor, to the needy, to fellow Christians.

Write the amount you're going to give into your budget. Decide exactly how much you believe you should give, then stick to it. "Each man should give what he has decided in his heart to give" (2 Corinthians 9:7).

Hmmm . . . so what if you decide to give *nothing?* Sorry. If you have the ability to make money, you *also* have the ability to give to God and others. "Command them to do good, to be rich in good deeds, and to be generous and willing to share" (1 Timothy 6:18; see also 2 Corinthians 9:6).

Paying Taxes

We won't dwell on this one too much. It's pretty straightforward: You either pay your taxes or you're in trouble. Now, you should take advantage of every legal tax shelter that you can, but as a Christian, you must be honest when paying your taxes. "Give everyone what you owe him: If you owe taxes, pay taxes" (Romans 13:7). God blesses honesty.

Pay Your Basic Bills

Beginning with Housing, all percentages are based on your Net Spendable Income (NSI). So calculate 30 percent of your income (after giving and taxes) and write that dollar amount in the blank to the right of Housing. If your NSI is $1,000/month, write $300 in Housing. Your subcategories, from Mortgage to Other, should then add up to $300.

If you stick to the percentages we've outlined for each category, you should always have enough for every expense in your life. Nevertheless, we do suggest that you pay your basic bills before buying personal items. This means paying for housing, electricity, and food first of all. If an emergency happens and you aren't able to use 7 percent of your income for Entertainment/Recreation that month, well, at least you'd have *food*. If worse came to worse, you could play with your food.

About now you may be asking, "What if my bills for these categories are more than the recommended percentages?" These percentages are not carved in stone, but they *are* tested and they *do* work. If your bills are significantly higher—say, Housing takes up 45 percent of your income—we suggest you change your lifestyle. You can't budget more than 100 percent of your income, after all. (Of course, if you're living at home and Housing costs nothing, great! More money to put in Savings toward the things you *really* want and need.)

Filling in the Form

If you haven't already done so, make a couple photocopies of the *Monthly Income & Expenses* form we provided a few pages back, and practice filling in dollar amounts in the various categories. If, as we said before, your Net Spendable Income (NSI) is $1,000, then 30 percent means $300 for Housing, 17 percent means $170 for Food, etc.

After you've assigned dollar amounts to each category, then divide the money for each category into its subcategories. If you allocated $70 to Entertainment/Recreation, then every month you can spend $20 on meals out, $15 on trips, zero on baby-sitters, $15 on activities, put $10 toward your Vacation fund, and use the final $10 for "other."

Short-Term Savings Goals

The money for short-term savings goals does *not* come from the 5 percent Savings category. That is for long-term savings goals only. All short-term savings goals come from the other nine categories.

For example, if your NSI is $1,000/month, you can spend $50/month on Clothing. If you want a $100 leather jacket, you'll need to save up your Clothing money for two months. (Or save half of it for four months.) If you want a new couch, that must come out of the Other of your $300/month Housing budget.

If you put $10 of your Entertainment allowance into a Vacation fund every month, by the end of the year you'll have $120. Pool your money with friends and go on a one-week camping trip. Or if you want a $100 used guitar, either save your $10/month Other funds for ten months, or else cut back your other Entertainment spending and save $20/month for a guitar. A new stereo system would also fit under Entertainment savings goals. Get the picture?

Every year you have to buy birthday gifts and cards, right?—and Christmas presents every Christmas, right? Where does this money come from? It would come from your $60/month Miscellaneous category. Set aside $10/month for gifts, and you'll be able to spend $120 on gifts each year.

Long-Term Savings Accounts

We allocate 5 percent of income to Savings (long-term savings). It must be understood that that is simply a starting place. This is especially true when you are young with your whole life ahead of you: You need to start saving toward some serious long-term goals, and you need to save more than 5 percent of your NSI to reach them.

For the time being, however, refrain from cannibalizing your other budget categories. We'll show you how to leave them begging for mercy in chapter 4, but for now, stick to putting only 5 percent of your NSI a month into Long-Term Savings. On our sample budget, that's $50/month. This $50 must be divided between no less than six or seven different savings goals. That means you'll be putting $10/month toward some savings goals and only $5/month toward others. Don't worry, it can be made to work.

List of Savings Accounts

On page 26 is a form, *List of Savings Accounts*. Make two photocopies of this list; label one "Plan A," and—drawing the figures from your *Monthly Income & Expenses*—fill in the dollar amounts you've allocated to each category.

In chapter 5 we'll discuss short-term savings goals, and in chapter 6 we'll discuss long-term savings goals. At that time, with a clearer idea, you can take the second photocopy, label it "Plan B," and adjust the figures.

Here's an example: If you want a $100 used guitar, write $100 under *Total needed*, $10 under *Monthly deposit*, and 10 under *Months saved*. Another example: In chapter 6 "Where to Cut," we will show you how to save 12 percent of your income ($120) every month for a car. For now assume you're doing that. If you needed a car as soon as possible and had to make a $1,000 down payment, it would take you about seven months at $120/month to save up $1,000.

LIST OF SAVINGS ACCOUNTS

SHORT-TERM SAVINGS ACCOUNTS

Category	*Total needed*	*Monthly deposit*	*Months saved*
1. Gifts	$_____	$_____	Mos. =_____
2. Christmas Gifts	$_____	$_____	Mos. =_____
3. Clothing	$_____	$_____	Mos. =_____
4. Home (furniture, etc.)	$_____	$_____	Mos. =_____
5. Vacation	$_____	$_____	Mos. =_____
6. Other	$_____	$_____	Mos. =_____
7. Other	$_____	$_____	Mos. =_____

LONG-TERM SAVINGS ACCOUNTS

Category	*Total needed*	*Monthly deposit*	*Years saved*
1. Savings for a Car	$_____	$_____	Yrs. =_____
2. College (education)	$_____	$_____	Yrs. =_____
3. Wedding	$_____	$_____	Yrs. =_____
4. First Home	$_____	$_____	Yrs. =_____
5. Retirement Savings	$_____	$_____	Yrs. =_____
6. Urgent Giving	$_____	$_____	Yrs. =_____
7. Job Loss Funds	$_____	$_____	Yrs. =_____
8. Other	$_____	$_____	Yrs. =_____
TOTAL	**$_____**	**$_____**	

CHAPTER 4

Setting Up a Savings Account

"We go through this every time. I'm telling you...it's just as safe putting your money in the bank!"

Setting Up a Savings Account

Getting Started

Now that we've convinced you that you need to save—we *have*, haven't we?—the first thing to do is to make sure you have a safe place for your savings. The best place is a savings account, and many banks have made opening a savings account as easy as possible.

Banks want to encourage new and younger clients. Many banks today have banking programs designed for teens and even children. They also have programs and booklets designed for the beginning banker. They may also give out gifts as incentives. Most importantly, many junior savings accounts have a lower first deposit minimum, and a higher interest rate to encourage younger clients.

Setting up a savings account is not difficult. It's as simple as setting up a checking account, something you've probably already done. (We recommend that parents help their teens set up checking and savings accounts by age thirteen.) At any rate, by the time you were in high school, you very likely *had* opened a savings account and a checking account. If not, let's take care of that right now.

Take your time and pick a bank carefully. Don't go bursting through the doors of the nearest one to open an account without checking out several other banks first. (Important tip: If you've been out skiing, take off your ski mask before you run in. That bell going off is *not* ringing to let everyone know it's lunch break.)

Compare various banks' accounts and interest rates. Phone around and shop for the best deal. Your savings account will be an important tool to help you save money and keep track of it, and the right account will help you save the most money and will pay the most interest.

Once you've chosen a bank, make an appointment with a teller, take off the ski mask, and go in. Ask questions till you're

satisfied with the answers and you know how things work. You should ask questions such as:
- I plan on opening a short-term savings account and a long-term one. What different savings plans do you have?
- Do you have any brochures or booklets I can study?
- How much must I deposit to open a savings account?
- What is the interest rate?
- Do I need to maintain a minimum balance? How much?
- Are there monthly service charges? How much?
- How many checks a month can I write for free?
- How much does it cost for each check I write?

After filling out the forms and signing the papers, the teller will give you a bank card. She should also give you an account register. This last item will help you keep your deposits, withdrawals, and interest payments organized. And from here on in, the bank will send you account information in the mail. (Or you can get a passbook that you update at your bank or ATM.)

How *Many* Savings Accounts?

A good question is: "Should I open up just *one* savings account and keep all my money there, or should I have two or more savings accounts?"

We suggest that you open different savings accounts for your different types of savings plans. For example, you may want to "lock in" your retirement funds in a savings account where you promise not to take money out for many years, and for which the bank rewards you with a higher interest rate. (But see *Your First Investment* in this series for a better way to get ready for retirement.)

On the other hand, you'll probably want to withdraw money from your short-term savings account more often. (You don't want to wait till you retire to buy that new stereo, do you?) If you "lock in" short-term money with long-term savings, you'll pay a penalty when you withdraw it from that account. On the other hand, if you lump your long-term savings with your short-term savings, you'll be severely tempted to "borrow" your long-term cash. And you'll be earning less interest in a short-term account.

It's also wise to have a separate account for each major savings goal: education, a first home, and retirement. Depending on who gives you the best deal, these accounts may or may not even be with the same bank. We'll deal with different savings plans later, but for now . . .

You should open at *least* two savings accounts: one for short-term savings and another for long-term savings. If you insist on having just *one* savings account, you do so at your own risk. (We will not be responsible.)

Recording Transactions

Each time you deposit money into your account, record the transaction in a checkbook ledger. You simply *must* keep track of the money you deposit in (or withdraw from) your savings accounts. Since these *are* savings accounts, you'll hopefully have a lot more deposits than withdrawals. In fact, you will only withdraw money when you've reached a short-term goal.

Individual Account Sheets

The previous form, *List of Savings Accounts*, gave you a bird's-eye view of all your savings accounts at once. It allowed you to see how much you could allocate to each category without missing any. Now, the *Individual Account Sheet* will allow you to keep track of how much you are depositing toward each goal.

If you're saving money for a new couch that costs $300, and you put $50 a month into savings toward that goal, you'll be able to buy it in six months. This isn't as quick as buying it tomorrow on credit, but be encouraged to know that, by making faithful, steady deposits, you can actually reach your goals without paying high interest charges.

Here's how to keep track: Make several photocopies of the *Individual Account Sheet* page, punch holes in them, and keep them in a three-ring binder. Then write each savings goal—for

INDIVIDUAL ACCOUNT SHEET

Account Name	Monthly Allocation	1st Pay Period	2nd Pay Period

DATE	TRANSACTION	DEPOSIT	W/DRAW	BALANCE

Total Goal to Reach   Projected Date   Actual Date
$_____   _____   _____

example, New Couch—in the top left-hand corner above Account Name. Above Monthly Allocation write how much you will be saving toward this goal each month, and, in the bottom left, how much your total savings goal is. In the bottom center write the date you think you will have that money.

Then, as you deposit money in your savings accounts, record those figures on the *Individual Account Sheet* for each category. (Don't forget to recalculate your balance each time.) When you finally have the money saved up, write in the actual date you reached your goal. Then, and only then, withdraw the money, zero out the account, and buy the item you saved up for.

Here's a tip: As you're starting out saving, set yourself a goal that you can reach in a couple months. Make it something you'll really enjoy. Then, when you achieve the goal and plunk your cash down for your purchase, you'll be hooked on saving. You'll *know* it works and will be willing to keep doing it.

What do you do with the money you've been putting toward that now-achieved goal? Reallocate it to different savings. Or, if you have a new savings goal you want to put that money toward, now is the time to do it.

Do a separate account sheet for each category, even if you do keep several categories in the same account. For example, you most likely will keep all your short-term savings together. It's not worth opening a separate account for each of them, yet you *do* need to keep track of how much money is designated toward each item.

If you haven't done it yet, stop now and set up your *Individual Account Sheets* binder. You should also make a point of phoning around and finding out which bank is best for you. Make an appointment, go in, and—for starters—set up a short-term savings account.

CHAPTER 5
Short-Term Savings

Short-Term Savings

OK, you've got your accounts set up. It's time to take a closer look at your short-term savings goals. The money for all your short-term savings goals is in one account.

Wanting and Waiting

How can you stick to your budget and not get swept along with the mob of credit card lemmings hurling themselves off the cliff? Be content with what you have. Paul wrote from prison, "I have learned the secret of being content in any and every situation . . . whether living in plenty or in want" (Philippians 4:12).

You may see something you want *now,* but do you need it *now?* Instead of buying on credit or robbing your college fund, save, wait a couple of months, then buy it with cash. That way, you *earn* interest while you save instead of *paying* 12 to 18 percent interest on credit card charges.

Make It a Goal

Never buy things on credit. If you really want something, make it a savings goal, then buy it with cash. For example, you want the Foghorn Boys' newest CD but you've already used up your Entertainment funds. Do you want that CD badly enough to make it a savings goal and wait a couple months to buy it?

Want that leather jacket? Long for designer jeans? They'll blow your Clothing allowance to bits unless you turn them into savings goals. Forget dipping into a first-come-first-served slush fund. Instead, write down a specific list of short-term goals, prioritize what you need or want the most, and ditch the rest. Or save them for later . . . much later.

And remember, just because the Foghorn Boys CD is a savings goal doesn't mean the next wad of cash in your short-term savings account goes toward it! *Only* the money saved in your Entertainment category does.

Getting Goodies Sooner

Of course, if you just *have* to have that CD or you'll die, you *can* move it up the priority list and use the money that you were saving for that cool jacket. If you don't mind waiting an extra couple months for the jacket, go buy the CD. You might miss a sale on that jacket, but *hey,* you live with your choices.

Don't make priority changes lightly. If you keep snatching money from other savings goals to buy goodies, your "new savings goals" are probably just *impulse buys* slamming like torpedoes into the soft underbelly of your budget.

- *Extra work:* Remember, there are other ways to get money so you can buy things you need. You can sell something you own, or you can take on an extra part-time job. Normally, having more money is *not* the solution. Being content and budgeting the money you *do* have is the solution. Nevertheless, there will be times you desperately need something, and you might have to take on extra work to earn the money you need.

- *Windfalls:* You should also set yourself a guideline as to how you will allocate unexpected money. A good guideline would be to say that if you receive any cash windfalls, you won't put all that money to one goal, but will divide it up something like this: 10 percent to giving, 40 percent to spending, 50 percent to savings. You can put a full 40 percent of unexpected money toward your most urgent goal, but only the portion of the 50 percent that is actually earmarked for your new goal.

Birthdays and Christmas

Many of you enjoy spending money on gifts. It's a way to say you care. Or you may belong to families where you're *expected* to buy presents—and though price tags are politely removed before wrapping, the gift's value is also politely appraised once the wrapping is ripped away.

So what do you do? If you don't want people to think you're Ebenezer Scrooge, you might pull out your credit card, charge it to the max, and carry a debt load. Not wise. No one will call you Scrooge, true, but they *might* think you look like Jacob Marley, dragging chains of debt around.

Where should gift money come from? From the Gifts (incl. Christmas) subcategory of Miscellaneous.

Juggle Your Accounts

The long and short of it is that anything you want, that you can't get with money earmarked for it in its budget category, needs to become a savings goal. Each time you add a goal with its *Individual Account Sheet*, you need to make room for it among your other goals and allocate funds to it. That means prioritizing your goals. High priority goals get money first.

You might have to reach your savings goal on another item or two before your newest goal can get any money allocated to it. For example, say you're already saving for a $100 tennis racket, a $300 stereo, and $60 designer jeans—in that order. You've allocated money so that you'll have the tennis racket by June, in time for summer, and the stereo by September. Now you want to add the "Best of the Foghorn Boys" double CD collection ($45).

You do some thinking and realize that you must have the tennis racket by June so the Foghorn Boys CD gets no money till June 15. At that point you'll take some of the money that used to go toward the racket and put it toward the stereo and the Foghorn Boys CD. The good news is you'll have the Foghorn Boys CD by August. The bad news is you won't get the stereo to play it on until October. *Great planning*.

Get the picture? It's a juggling game and you're the juggler. You have to decide which balls get thrown up in which order . . . and then catch them and rejuggle on schedule.

Take the time right now to prioritize your short-term savings goals. Look at when you need each item by and figure out how much you need to save toward your newest goal between now and that date. Then see how it fits in with all your other goals and dollar allocations. And rejuggle again . . .

CHAPTER 6

Long-Term Savings

Long-Term Savings

Long-Term Accounts

Long-term savings accounts are great! The bank not only pays you interest, it pays compound interest. That's interest on your interest. But *first* you need to keep your money in the bank long enough to gather interest. That's when long-term savings accounts can really put some moss on the rock.

There are several long-term goals that you should save towards. These include a car, college, your wedding, your first house, and retirement.

- *Chunky minimum deposits:* Banks often want a substantial minimum deposit for certain types of accounts such as a Registered Education Savings Plan, an Individual Retirement Account (or Registered Retirement Savings Plan), and a Home Owners Savings Plan. You have to plunk down a chunk to start these, but they really snowball after a while.

  You usually need $1,000 to open long-term accounts that pay higher interest. Save that deposit in your short-term account as a separate savings goal. Then, when you have enough, use it to open a long-term account. And do it again.

  Also, youth accounts are often designed for long-term saving. The bank likes you to leave your money with them a long time. They make plans for it and reward you with a higher interest rate. It's a good deal. You earn lots of money on your deposit and the bank uses it for a long time.

- *CDs—Certificates of Deposits:* When you save, the idea is to get the best rate of interest for your dollars. CDs do that. You and your bank agree on a certain amount of money for you to deposit. You agree on how long you will leave that money with them. You *must* leave your money in for the agreed time. No taking it out or there will be substantial penalties. (Some banks have removed or lowered the penalty, or reduced the minimum time.)

You could call this a guaranteed investment certificate. The bank guarantees that it will give you a good interest rate, keep your money safe, and give you back your money plus interest at the end of the time period. You guarantee that you'll leave your money in the bank until the time period is up. They then give you a higher interest rate. Sort of like, "I'll scratch your back if you'll scratch mine."

Let's look at the various long-term savings goals in the order that most people spend the money for them.

Saving for a Car

According to J. D. Power & Associates (an international market research firm), a new car costs, on the average, about $19,000 and a *good* secondhand car costs approximately $10,000. For teens and young adults, this is just about the biggest expense you'll have.

The more money you can come up with for a down payment, the less you'll have to pay in financing charges. If you buy a used car for $10,000 but only put 10 percent ($1,000) down, you'll have to finance the rest, probably financing $9,000 at 12 percent interest. What will you end up paying the bank? The $9,000 they loaned you, *plus* $1,768 in interest. You could have kept that $1,768 if you'd saved up money first, *then* bought a car. So does it make sense to save money? You betcha. It just means being car-less a little longer. But the exercise will do you good.

Saving for College

It might seem that saving for college belongs in the chapter about short-term savings. If you're about to graduate from high school or have already graduated, your plans to go to college will seem imminent, not long-term. Nevertheless, this *is* a long-term goal because of the hefty mountain of money you need to save for it, like, would you believe, $30,000 to $40,000?

How do you get your hands on that much money? Most teens take out a student loan. They figure they'll be earning lots of cash after they get their degree and will be able to pay it off easily. Instead, most of them end up in financial bondage. They not only have to pay the original amount, but the interest charges can balloon their debt by up to 10 percent a year! Ouch!

So how do you pay for it? We cover this subject fully in another book in the series, *Preparing for College*, but for now, we suggest that you take two years off before heading to college. Enter the workforce, save money, and put it in a long-term, high interest account. Besides, this will make you value your education more. You'll probably study harder, do better, and maybe land a better job.

However, it will still take decades to save $40,000 if your total allotment for *all* long-term savings is only 5 percent. So what do you do? Look into grants or scholarships. They could greatly reduce the amount of money you need. But if you're still short, well . . . you'll have to cut somewhere. We cover this later in the chapter.

Saving for Your Wedding

You may protest that weddings are too expensive and say, "I'll go for a simple wedding. Just the two of us and the minister, barefoot on the beach. I'll buy a ring from a pawn shop. Honeymoon? Uncle Elmer will let us stay in that cabin near his pig farm." *Right,* buddy! Have I got news for *you!* With a "wedding" like that, the honeymoon is already over.

However, most weddings *are* too extravagant. People saddle themselves with debt by throwing a megabash that they're still paying for years later. The average cost for a wedding in the U.S. today is a whopping $20,000. That includes not only the invitation cards but the wedding dress, bridesmaids' dresses, tuxedos, flowers, photographers, wedding cake, and on and on.

The most expensive part of the wedding is the reception that follows the ceremony. For two hundred guests, for hall rental, food, and catering, you'll pay over $8,000! The second biggest expense is the engagement ring, which usually costs over $3,000. And guess what? That $20,000 total doesn't even include the honeymoon! That adds thousands more dollars to the price tag!

A lot of young couples start down the road of debt together before they even say, "I do." Fully 80 percent of all divorces today are caused by financial problems and far too many marriage breakups begin with the wedding itself.

You can—and *should*—trim a lot of the cost off your wedding by trimming your guest list and expenses, but the point is: Your wedding is *still* going to be expensive, and you need to start saving for it today.

Buying a House

This expense used to hit at the same time as the wedding. Obviously, when people got married, they needed a place to live. These days, however, couples usually spend a minimum of four years in apartments or rented houses before making the down payment on their first home. There's nothing wrong with that. It's just the way things are. Overall, you're looking at a first house that will cost, on a national average, about $100,000.

You can finance that with a mortgage, but buying a home involves much more than just paying the mortgage each month. First, it is necessary to save up enough money for your down payment (usually 10–20 percent of the sale price) as well as the fees and closing costs (another 2–5 percent).

Where you borrow the money for your new home can make a big difference to its cost. The traditional sources are savings and loan (S&L) companies, banks, the government, and private lenders. However, there are usually several government programs available to first-time or low-income home buyers that provide loans at lower interest rates. The most widely known are: the Federal Housing Authority (FHA), the Veterans Administration (VA), and the Housing and Urban Development (HUD). Sometimes state or even local governments will aid first-time home buyers.

As we mentioned, the initial down payment is usually 10 percent of the total cost. How do you get that money? You save! You open a savings account, such as a Home Owners Savings Plan, for that purpose. Phone different banks and ask what kind of plan they have to offer.

The cost of your first home will depend on where you live. Location, location, location. For example, Seattle is expensive, whereas Cactus, Texas, is cheap. So you could be paying between $50,000 and $200,000 for the same home, depending on where you live. And if you live in Grizzly Creek in the Yukon, you can nearly have a home for free! Just build it out of pine trees like the beavers do.

Saving for Retirement

Retirement savings are crucial, yet most Americans neglect it. After a lifetime of work, the average sixty-five-year-old American has a net worth of $100 and depends entirely upon old age pension. That's why most senior citizens are so careful with how they spend their money. They barely have enough to pay the rent, buy food, and . . . well, that's it.

The only way to meet more than your most basic needs at retirement is to set aside money in a retirement fund. You're thinking: "I just got my first full-time job, and I'm supposed to plan for my retirement?" Yes. Start as early as possible. You do want to go to *Tahiti* one day, don't you? Well, the earlier you put money into a retirement plan, the faster it'll build. Hey! Forget Tahiti! By the time you retire, you'll be able to vacation on Mars. (For further details on investing for retirement, see the book *Your First Investment*.)

If you're putting funds aside for retirement, place them where you can't get at them easily. Why? Because when you "desperately" need money, which is the first savings account you'll go for? The one you won't need till the distant future. Since most young adults believe they will *never* get old, retirement funds will be the first to go.

Check with different banks about their Individual Retirement Accounts or Registered Retirement Savings Plans. Shop around for the best rates. Then, starting now, put a set percentage of your paycheck into a retirement savings fund every month. As you get better jobs and bigger paychecks, continue putting that same percentage into your Retirement Fund or even increase it as you grow older. Then, by the time you retire you'll be able to blast off. Literally.

Annuities are very popular investments for retirement planning. There are two basic types, fixed and variable. Go for variable. It's better for younger people who can't project what their money will be worth at retirement. If you put money into an annuity, read all about it beforehand.

A tip: Put money toward your Retirement Plan as early as possible. Considering the incredible snowball effect of compound interest, you should get several thousand dollars in that account as early as possible. It's better to ride the bus for years than to miss making deposits into your Retirement Fund.

The True North and RRSPs

Now let's talk about Canada. If you live north of the 49th Parallel, you have heard of RRSPs (Registered Retirement Savings Plan). This is a nifty little tax shelter that the federal government has set up for its citizens. Every year before tax season, Canadians can put a certain amount of money into RRSPs. They then don't pay tax on that amount. Great, eh?

The problem is, millions of Canadians *don't* take advantage of it. The government begs: "Please don't pay us taxes! Put it into your retirement fund!" But what do Canadians do? They spend their spare money at Christmas instead of buying RRSPs. Then, come tax time, they grumble about "government waste" as they scrape money together to pay taxes. And they wonder why they can't retire their dogsled or upgrade their igloo.

Where to Cut

Now the $50 question: How do you divvy up the money in your 5 percent Savings category? (Since in our sample budget 5 percent is $50, this really is a $50 question.) It will take you a *looooonng* time to save for college, for example, if all you can put toward it is $10/month. Here's where you need to look around at other categories for spare cash.

Look at Miscellaneous. This includes everything from Toiletries to Lunches, and gets 6 percent of your income. It also includes Special Education. Say you cut back on

Toiletries (not *too* much, please!) and put a full 3 percent toward Education. That helps, but not enough. Obviously, you'll need to cut back in other areas too.

Let's look at Housing and Food: Housing is 30 percent of your budget and Food, 17 percent for a total of 47 percent. What if your parents take pity on you and let you pay 20 percent of your income for room and board? Put the other 27 percent toward college. See if you can also cut back on Clothing, Auto expenses, and Recreation. Every little bit helps, and as expensive as college is, you'll *need* to save as much as you can!

We also suggest you use 5 percent of your income to pay debts. If you have none, put it all into savings as well!

If you can cut a percentage or two from other categories and put *that* into long-term savings, go for it. For example, if you don't own a car, set aside enough for bus fare then put the rest into savings. If you only spend 3 percent of your income on buses, taxis, and bicycle chains every month, that lets you put a whopping 12 percent into savings. Put it toward your first car, or your college education.

You might want to buy your clothes in thrift stores and spend 2 percent of your NSI—not 5—on clothing. There's a savings of 3 percent. Just don't be so tight that you save everything and leave nothing in other categories.

Don't eliminate the 7 percent Entertainment/Recreation category entirely and sit in the dark, muttering over your gruel like Ebenezer Scrooge. You need to relax. Live too Spartan and you'll get so frustrated that one day you'll go crazy and completely lose it. So give a priority to fun.

It's up to you to figure out how much you can cull from your other categories for long-term savings. Why not take the time right now to do some number crunching?

And now, let's have a look at the last few categories in your Long-term Savings categories. After this you'll be ready to return to your *List of Savings Accounts* on page 26 and write out your final figures.

CHAPTER 7
Saving for Emergencies

Saving for Emergencies

Contingency Funds

You've decided on your short- and long-term savings goals and are saving away. Nickel by nickel, dime by dime, dollar by dollar, you're building up your savings. Everything's covered, right? Well, not *quite*.

Emergencies happen whether we plan for them or not. So it makes sense to plan ahead and have funds in your budget to meet them. What happens if a $500 emergency hits and there's not a penny to take care of it? Out comes the credit card, up goes the debt, and your budget looks like someone took a shotgun to it from close range. Or else you're forced to draw money from your Education Fund or Wedding Fund.

Contingency plans exist to cover things like major car repairs, household disasters, urgent charitable giving, losing your job, etc. So how much should you set aside in a Contingency Fund? First, study your past expenses and make an educated guess on the amount of money you'll need for each contingency category.

You may feel overwhelmed at the sheer number of savings categories that your paltry 5 percent Savings has to cover. You may wonder, "How is it *possible* to get so much mileage out of 5 percent of my income?" Well, it's *not*. But don't despair. Many Contingency Funds are subcategories of other budget categories. For example . . .

Auto Repairs

If you will look at the *Monthly Income & Expenses* chart on page 21, you'll notice that most contingencies are already covered in one of the twelve expense categories. For example, Maintenance/Repair/Replacement is included under Auto(s) and is part of the 15 percent of your Net Spendable Income. If you've been faithfully putting a percentage into Repair, then when your transmission gives up the ghost and you need a new one, you'll have the funds. It won't take the sting out of paying all that cash, but at least you'll be *able* to pay. (Saving up for repairs is covered in detail in another book in this series, *Buying Your First Car*.)

Insurance

Some Christians believe that buying insurance of any kind shows a lack of trust in God. After all, if you're God's child, nothing bad can happen to you, right? Wrong. God's Word teaches that God will provide for you, *not* that He will protect you from every accident. God expects you to do your part, as well. That's why Proverbs 27:12 says, "The prudent see danger and take refuge, but the simple keep going and suffer for it."

A good way for the prudent to "take refuge" is to buy insurance. Far too many Christians who didn't take out insurance certainly did "suffer for it" when they had a major accident. All their plans and dreams were put on hold while they paid high bills they never imagined they'd have.

It is true, however, in the U.S. today, many people over-insure. They insure against everything from the kitchen sink cracking to an attack by Martians. They insure themselves so heavily that they no longer feel a need to pray for God's protection. But remember, it's the misuse of insurance, the overdependence upon insurance, that is wrong. Insurance itself is not unscriptural.

- *Auto insurance:* It's *fortunate* that auto insurance is required by law. If it weren't, millions of Christians would "save money" by not buying it and end up in debt after a collision. As it is, their insurance rates shoot up, but it's a lot better than going bankrupt paying for someone else's medical bills. This is another point: Your auto insurance exists to help pay for second and third party injuries as well. Don't make someone else suffer for your shortsightedness.

- *Life/medical insurance:* Apart from Home and Auto Insurance, we advocate putting 5 percent of your income into category six, Life Insurance and Medical Insurance. You may not feel you need life insurance right now, but it's wise to get it. You will definitely need insurance after you're married and certainly once you have children. If you have a debilitating accident but don't die, you'll need insurance to help pay the bills.

As a young person, you're far better off buying *term* insurance instead of *whole life* insurance. Term insurance needs to be constantly renewed and the price goes up at the beginning of each new period, but if you are short on cash, term insurance will not only be the less expensive choice but your *only* choice.

We advocate getting medical insurance as well; otherwise, if you have an accident or an extended illness, you will be saddled with debt trying to pay hospital bills. For the same reason, we recommend that you buy home insurance to protect yourself against theft, fires, or other damage. (See the section Housing on *Monthly Income & Expenses*.) Insurance makes sense. Just stay within your budget. Don't buy more insurance than you need.

Household Contingencies

A Household Contingency Fund covers everything from a neon light that needs to be replaced to your fridge giving up the ghost, to calling in cleaners after a five-hour food fight in your flat. However, if you rent an apartment (and forbid food fights), then your expenses should be minimal. Most utility repairs will be the landlord's responsibility anyway.

Saving for household contingencies should be included in the Housing category under Maintenance. As a young adult living at home or in a rental unit, this may not be an issue for you. If you're a young couple living in your own home, it would be very wise to have a few thousand dollars saved for household contingencies.

Saving for Job Loss

One of the most practical reasons to have money in savings is to cover living costs if you lose your job. Job changes are a part of life these days. The paychecks may stop coming but the bills don't, and income or no, you'll still need to pay the rent, eat, and put gas in your car. How will you pay for these things? (a) Use money you've put in savings for just such an event? Or (b) use your credit card and rack up debt?

If you had a full-time job and were laid off (you didn't quit and weren't fired), after several weeks of being without a job, your Unemployment Insurance will kick in. But how do you survive until it does? (Apart from moving back in with your parents that is.) Also, many jobs available for young adults are part-time labor, which means you *won't* be receiving U.I. when your job ends. If you have no savings, you'll be forced to take the scummiest jobs around, just to earn money.

If you have set aside money in a Job Loss Fund, however, then you'll be able to draw on it. You should also use your short-term savings goals at this time. After all, what do you need most, that new $200 coat or food? The only savings accounts you shouldn't touch are your long-term savings. Leave *that* money there, unless, of course, the lean times just go on and on and on.

Over the years, Crown Financial Ministry (CFM) counselors have talked with many couples who were going through tough times because of job losses. Many of these couples actually had savings accounts but were borrowing money to live on instead of using their savings. When they were asked why, they said they didn't want to use their savings because they needed the *security*. They'd rather go into debt than spend their savings. In reality, they weren't saving; they were hoarding.

Urgent Charitable Giving

What if it's not *you* that loses your job, but a single mom? What if your pastor asks those who can to give to meet her family's need? Or what do you do when you've been witnessing to a family and their house burns down? What do you do when you hear of intense persecution of Christians in another country? Or if a Christian relief organization makes an urgent appeal for funds? Well, if you don't have a penny set aside, you'll be tempted to go into debt to help them. That's not wise.

The wisest course of action is to have funds *already* set aside in an Emergency Giving Fund. Include this as part of your Charitable Giving budget. Remember, you don't have to be limited to giving only 10 percent of your income. The early Christians freely gave to help others. In A.D. 197, the Christian apologist, Tertullian of Carthage, wrote about Christian giving in his treatise, *Apologeticum*.

> On the monthly day, if he likes, each puts in a small donation; but only if it be his pleasure, and only if he be able. These gifts are . . . to support and bury poor people, to supply the wants of boys and girls destitute of means and parents, and of old persons confined now to the house; such, too, as have suffered shipwreck and if there happen to be any in the mines, or banished to the islands, or shut up in the prisons, for nothing but their fidelity to the cause of God's Church.

Some Christians have received a special gift of giving (Romans 12:8). To them, saving money means having more to share with others; so they put money in the bank, let it collect interest, then use it when a need touches their hearts. You might consider doing this. It's great to respond to needs, but it's even *more* wonderful to *plan* to respond to them.

We have now explained the last few categories on your long-term savings plans. What do you do with this info? Remember the *List of Savings Accounts* we had you fill out in chapter 3? Well, now you can adjust the figures on "Plan A," pick up the blank "Plan B," and fill in all the lines with more realistic figures.

CHAPTER 8

Nickels and Dimes

Nickels and Dimes

When You Don't Have Much

Now that you've seen how far your paltry budget needs to stretch and how many needs there are to save for, you may be overwhelmed and be tempted to think, "Fine, I'll start saving when I'm older, have a better job, and am earning more. Right now I'm dog-paddling to pay bills and barely keeping my head above water. What little I *could* put in savings at this point isn't worth it."

Wrong. First of all, what a person puts off till tomorrow often doesn't get done. Ever. This ties into the second reason: If you start to save now, even if you can only spare a few dollars from each paycheck, you establish a lifelong habit. You learn to discipline yourself, exercise self-control over your spending habits, and practice saving instead of spending.

Even if you don't have much, you can still save money by cutting back in simple ways. For example, do you *really* need to pay $3.50 twice a day for an overpriced, frothy double latte, or can you get by with a sixty-cent regular down at the corner? Do you really need the newest computer game when you already have five computer games and haven't read your Bible in a month?

The third reason for saving when you're poor is because it's a scriptural principle. Proverbs 13:11 says, "He who gathers money little by little makes it grow." This is where the money's made—in the nickels and dimes. This is *also* where it's usually lost. "A poor man's field may produce abundant food, but injustice sweeps it away" (Proverbs 13:23). Too often, "injustice" describes the way people sack and pillage their own resources.

Interest and Compound Interest

Also bear in mind that your money (little as it might be) is *worth* more early in the game. That is, the sooner you start saving, the sooner interest begins building up on your deposit, and compound interest on top of that. That's why, when saving for retirement, it's smarter to start young and steadily save money than it is to drop in a large amount later on in life. You will have missed out on all that interest building up over the years.

Just as small, consistent deposits of money add up to huge savings, consistent right decisions add up to a lifetime of right choices. Make all your small decisions according to God's principles, and that will make the big decisions easier. We're not only talking about being honest with the nickels and dimes—and that *is* important—but we're talking about getting into the habit of saving nickels and dimes when you're young. Start the habit early and it will stick with you for a lifetime. You won't regret it.

Saving While in Debt

Besides "treading water" to make ends meet, another reason people give for not saving is debt. The question has been asked: "We're working on a budget to get ourselves out of debt. We're also working on a repayment schedule with our creditors. Do we have the right to save while we still owe money to someone else?"

The answer is yes. *Every* person should allocate a percentage of his or her income to savings. If you don't have *any* savings and your car breaks down or the fridge quits, then you'll have to pay with a credit card and ultimately end up even deeper in debt. If you don't save, you probably *will* have to borrow again. Saving is really debt prevention.

Many times CFM counselors have had couples contact their creditors about negotiating lower monthly payments on debts. Often when a creditor reviewed their debtors' budgets—which included money set aside for savings—the creditor would call to ask why he or she should take reduced payments while the couple had savings. The counselor would respond, "Because they have made a commitment to no more debt. As long as they don't generate any more debt, you can be assured that they will pay what they have promised." Rarely has a creditor objected any further.

Personal Discipline

Earlier we quoted Proverbs 13:11, which says, "He who gathers money little by little makes it grow." But to be able to gather it little by little takes discipline. The terrific news is, however, that banks reward such diligence with compound interest that turns a small initial investment into a very large sum of money indeed.

A CFM counselor once talked with a pastor who had saved more than $250,000 during his forty years in the ministry, yet the highest salary he had ever earned was $10,000 a year. The counselor asked him, "Pastor, if you were to give counsel to a young person today on how to develop a surplus of money, what would it be?"

"It's simple," he said. "Always spend less than you make."

Even if your salary is small, as long as you're spending less than you make, you'll have money to set aside in savings. Developing a surplus is not difficult. All it requires is a little bit of money diligently saved over a long period of time. The issue is to have self-control, which the Bible says is a "fruit of the Spirit" (Galatians 5:23).

So, no matter what your situation is, make a commitment right now to save.

CHAPTER 9
Sticking to Your Plan

Sticking to Your Plan

How *Not* to Save Money

Now that you've mapped out a plan for saving and understand the needs you will be saving for, it should be easy to save. You put money into your savings account every two weeks or month, and presto, your savings multiply! Right?

Wrong. This is *not* usually what happens for two reasons: First, people want what they want—now. Every want is a "need" and every covetous desire is a necessity. Often their savings accounts will be empty because they don't believe in saving enough to save one dollar in the first place.

The second reason is that even when they *do* put money into savings, they lack the willpower to *keep* it there. When the money in their checking account is gone on rent, food, and other bills, an unbudgeted expense comes along—a new wardrobe, or a TV on sale. Their response? They dip into their savings with nary a twinge of conscience.

The logic? Their present "need" is so great or the deal so good that they *have* to have it now. They say, "I can always put the money back into savings, but a deal like this doesn't happen every day." *Sure* they can put money back. And take it out again just as quickly. And put it back in. And . . .

Don't believe us? It's this easy: You go to pay for an item and that little handheld thingie asks: Checking or Savings? Of course you press Checking. But if the message says, *Insufficient Funds,* what do you do? Sigh and put the item back, thinking, "I don't have the money"? If you were born in North America anywhere above the Rio Grande, chances are you will try again, and this time punch Savings.

Savings comes from the same root word as "safe," but "savings" that are only *one* button punch away from your fingers are *not* safe. The only way to save money is to put it in savings and *leave* it there. Don't touch it! How do you do that? Self-restraint. Saving is a matter of personal discipline.

Dipping into the Honey Pot

Remember Pooh Bear? He wasn't satisfied with just a bit of honey. He emptied honey pot after honey pot until he'd gobbled up Rabbit's entire supply. What is the moral here? Once you put money in savings, don't give in to the temptation to dip into it. You might not be able to stop.

If you have trouble keeping your hands out of your savings account, build yourself some safeguards. Make sure you can't access your savings account from your debit card. If you have to, literally keep them in two separate banks and never go near the savings bank unless you're depositing money or withdrawing it for a legitimate saved-up-for expense. Do that and you will save. Guaranteed!

Tax Refunds

Too many Christians treat a tax refund like a gift from Uncle Sam with a note attached: "Treat yourself! Go wild!" Believe it or not, a tax refund is not an "unexpected windfall." It is not a gift that appeared by surprise out of nowhere, with no rules on how it should be spent. If you've been tracking your finances and have filled out your tax forms correctly, you *knew* it was coming. That money did not appear out of a hat—Uncle Sam's hat or the Cat in the Hat's hat. It is directly tied to your hard work just like every other dollar you earn, and should be budgeted the same. Decide *before* it arrives exactly how much you'll save, for which goal, how much you'll spend, and on what.

When You *Shouldn't* Give

You should always give to God, even if you're poor and can't give much. But once you've given that, what about *extra* giving to needy causes? In the last chapter we talked about saving money "that [we] may have something to share with those in need" (Ephesians 4:28).

But what about times when you yourself are "in need"? You might not be ready to pass around a hat, but you also may not have much left to give. So should you give anyway? No. God doesn't expect you to feel obligated to meet every single need you encounter, especially if you are poor.

Let's say Missionary Bob asks you to give $35 a month to help him fly around teaching. You're struggling to make ends meet, have a $25,000 college loan to repay, live in a small apartment, are working for near minimum wage, and are *already* giving to a missionary. You still feel that tug on your heart. But if you give more than $10 as a one time gift, you'll blow your budget to shreds. What to do?

Paul exhorted the Christians of Corinth to give. He praised the Philippians for giving even in their poverty. (See 2 Corinthians 8:1–4.) But he also made it clear that if people just did not have the money to give, they *shouldn't* give. It is not God's will for the tenderhearted and the generous to give every time they're asked, leaving them hard-pressed—so that others then have to help *them* out.

"For if the willingness is there, the gift is acceptable according to what one *has*, not according to what he does *not* have. Our desire is not that others might be relieved while you are hard pressed" (2 Corinthians 8:12–13, emphasis added).

Make a Deal

Finally, what do you do when you see the buy of the century in a store window, and its magnetic pull is so strong that it slams you up against the glass and practically sucks the credit card from your wallet? What do you do when the siren song of its price tag nearly causes you to ram the ship of your budget up onto the reefs of debt?

As you peel your face off the glass, make a deal with yourself. Tell yourself this: "I will not buy this irresistible item right now. I won't. I'm going to go home. I'm going to go home and wait forty-eight hours. Then, if I *still* absolutely have to have it, I'll write it into my financial plan. I'll budget the money to buy it."

Do this and you'll be amazed at how impulse buying can be brought under control. A day or two can make most magnetic "must haves" lose their grip over your mind and your money.

CHAPTER 10

The Payoff

The Payoff

Small Beginnings
If you haven't been used to living within a budget and money has been flowing out of your wallet like water from a burst fire hydrant, it will take time to bring your spending habits under control. (You have five minutes.) You may also be discouraged when you open several accounts at one time, but only have a few dollars to drop into each one. Don't worry, in time you'll build up savings. (You have five decades.)

If you fine-tune the budget in this book to meet your saving needs, "your beginnings will seem humble, so prosperous will your future be" (Job 8:7). Also, "he who gathers money little by little makes it grow" (Proverbs 13:11). This is especially true with modern banks, where your money earns interest and even your interest earns interest.

Most of all, remember the ant. Rome wasn't built in a day, and neither was an anthill. If you were a hungry aardvark and had the inclination to rip open an anthill, you would find its subterranean larders filled to overflowing with grain and other goodies that the ants carried there grain by grain over long periods of time. These things take time.

Make a Plan Today
We hope you have enjoyed this book, but behind the humor is a call to self-control and self-denial. This book is a bugle blast badgering you to build a budget, live a budget, and stick to a budget. It is a clarion call to control your cravings, cache your credit card, tune out the siren call of "gotta have it" ads, and block out the "lust of [the] eyes" (1 John 2:16).

It's true that "you're only young once." But remember, you'll be old all the *rest* of the time. (Well, *older* at least.) The stewardship habits you form now could save you years of pain later and thousands and thousands of dollars. The steps you take now will be permanently recorded in the cement sidewalk of adulthood.

Be Accountable

If you have a history of not living within a budget and feel you might fall captive to your old sinful ways again, safeguard your savings by making yourself accountable. Show your written plan to your mom or dad, or to someone you trust. Tell them exactly what percentage of your earnings you plan on putting into each savings category. Let them know that you may be tempted to blow your budget, raid your savings, and fail to deposit, and that you want to be accountable about your accounts. Give them permission to question and even hound you . . . and promise to listen!

Taking Stock

You're not quite done yet. Starting your plan is the beginning, but it's not the end, so don't lose this book! We suggest that one year from the time you implement a budget and begin saving, you take stock of how closely you have stuck to your budget. Pull out your *Individual Account Sheets* to see exactly how much you have squirreled away in each of your savings accounts. Then compare that to your plan.

If you have kept an accurate record of all your deposits, you'll also know exactly how much interest you have earned in your savings accounts. It might not be a lot at the end of the first year, but wait and watch it snowball.

If you haven't measured up to your plan, reread this book and see where you could have done better. Perhaps you need to still rein in your spending habits so that you're not living beyond your means or buying on credit. Or if you find that your plan was too ambitious and unrealistic, don't get down. Just adjust your plan. But whatever you do, keep saving and being wise as an ant.

Glossary

Allocating funds: To deliberately earmark a specific amount of money for a designated savings goal.

Appreciation: To increase in value.

Budget: A specific, written plan where you allot a percentage of your income to each category of bills and expenses before you get the money. (*See also* Net Spendable Income)

Compound interest: Interest that is calculated daily. This is interest upon the interest.

Contingency funds: Savings to be used in the event of an emergency, or a sudden, urgent need (contingency).

Hoarding: Gathering more material goods than you need, whether motivated by greed or a lack of trust in God.

Interest: Money you pay for the privilege of borrowing money.

Long-term savings: When you save thousands of dollars for years (or a lifetime) to meet very large savings goals.

Net Spendable Income (NSI): Money left over from your paycheck after charitable giving and taxes. You then budget this NSI into the various categories.

Prioritizing: Putting a priority on a need or want, depending on how soon you want or need that item.

Savings goals: A written need or want that you regularly deposit money toward. You use that money to purchase the item when you reach your goal (have the money you need).

Short-term savings: When you save tens or hundreds of dollars for weeks or months to meet a smaller savings goal.

Surplus: Anything above and beyond your regular supply; extra, leftover money.

Index

accountable 61
accounts, savings 28–32
    separate 30–32
    setting up 28–29
allocating funds 30–31
annuities 43
auto, buying 10, 25, 39, 44
bills, basic 23
budget 20, 60–61
Certificates of Deposit (CDs) 38–39
college 11, 39–40, 43–44
compound interest 43, 52–54
contingency funds, 46–50
credit cards 15–17
cutting back 23, 43–44
debt 10, 14, 16, 44, 53
emergencies 23, 46–50
entertainment/recreation 23, 24, 34, 44
gifts 24, 35–36
giving
    charitable 22, 35
    urgent 49–50
    when not to 57–58
hoarding 9–10, 49
home, buying
    down payment 11, 41
    mortgage 11, 23, 41–42
impulse buying 16–17, 20, 35, 58
Individual Account Sheets 30–32, 36, 61
insurance 47–48
interest 16, 38, 39, 43, 52–54
job loss 48–49
List of Savings Accounts 25–26, 50
minimum deposit 28
Monthly Income & Expenses 20–25
needs, meeting 9, 10
Net Spendable Income (NSI) 23–24
principal 16
prioritizing 35–36
Registered Education Savings Plan (RESP) 38
Registered Retirement Savings Plans (RRSP) 38, 43
retirement 11, 21, 42–43
saving
    little by little 52–54, 60
    scriptural 8–10, 14–15
savings goals
    long-term 10, 24–25, 29–30, 38–44
    short-term 10, 24, 29–30, 34–36
self-denial/discipline 17, 23, 34, 52, 54, 57, 58, 60
spending, unwise 14–17, 20, 56–57
stewardship 60
taking stock 61
taxes 22
tax refunds 57
trusting God 9
wedding, saving for 11, 40–41
windfalls 35, 57

building Christian faith in families

Lightwave Publishing is one of North America's leading developers of quality resources that encourage, assist, and equip parents to build Christian faith in their families. Lightwave's products help parents answer their children's questions about the Christian faith, teach them how to make church, Sunday school, and Bible reading more meaningful for their children, provide them with pointers on teaching their children to pray, and much, much more.

Lightwave, together with its various publishing and ministry partners, such as Focus on the Family, has been successfully producing innovative books, music, and games since 1984. Some of its more recent products include the *Parents' Guide to the Spiritual Growth of Children*, *My Time With God*, and *Mealtime Moments*.

Lightwave also has a fun kids' Web site and an Internet-based newsletter called *Tips and Tools for Spiritual Parenting*. For more information and a complete list of Lightwave products, please visit: **www.lightwavepublishing.com**.

A MINISTRY OF MOODY BIBLE INSTITUTE

Moody Press, a ministry of Moody Bible Institute, is designed for education, evangelization, and edification.

If we may assist you in knowing more about Christ and the Christian life, please write us without obligation:

Moody Press, c/o MLM, Chicago, Illinois 60610

Or visit us at Moody's Web site: **www.moodypress.org**